123

by Lesley Clark
photography by Garie Hind

Ladybird

 one

one teddy bear

2 two

two boots

3 three

three cars

four

four ducks

5 five

five toothbrushes

6 six

six building blocks

7 seven

seven paint pots

8 eight

eight apples

 nine

nine boats

Encourage your child to point to each boat as she counts it.

10 ten

ten socks

Count the socks and try to match the pairs on the line. You could do this at home with real socks or other objects.

What can you see in this bag?

How many of each thing?

Can you help to unpack
the shopping?

Is everything here?

Here's the washing to sort out.

Let's get everything out of the basket.

How many T-shirts can you count?

How many socks?

Each of these boxes has three ducks in it. Can you count them?

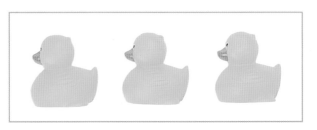

Play games with buttons and other objects to help your child to understand that the number stays the same no matter how the objects are arranged.

How many drinks are there?

Is there a straw for each drink?

How many horses are on the farm?

How many cows?

How many geese?

Count up all the animals and say
how many there are altogether.

These four cars drive round
and round.

These four are home –
safe and sound.

What games do you play with
your cars?

How many balls?

Which is the largest?

Which is the smallest?

Talk about the different sizes and colours of the balls.

Can you count how many flowers?

Which one is different from all the others?

Yum! How many green diamonds are on the cake?

How many red diamonds?

How many diamonds are there altogether?

first steps with ladybird

First steps with ladybird is a range of mini readers, activity books and flash cards designed to develop the essential early skills of children aged 2 and upwards.

Mini readers

These durable hardback books use photographs and illustrations to introduce important early learning concepts.

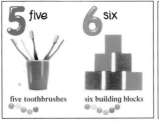

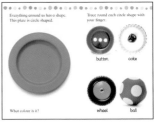